Contents

Robert Failla   Rainbow

Robert Failla   Rainbow

Robert Failla   Rainbow

Hipgnosis

Hipgnosis

Hipgnosis

Peter Watts, Road Manager interviewed by
Frank Torker

On the back cover of Ummagumma is a striking picture of
Pink Floyd's sound gear. Standing nonchalantly amongst the
speakers is Mr. Peter Watts, Pink Floyd's redoubtable road
manager. I spoke to him the day after one of their recent
gigs. It is 5 p.m., Sunday afternoon, May 1973.

Frank: How old are you Pete ?

Pete: Twenty-seven.

Frank: What's the official title of your job ?

Pete: Road Manager.

Frank: What does that entail ?

Pete: It entails being in charge of getting everything
together for them so that all they have to do is just walk on
stage and play.

Frank: How long have you been doing that ?

Pete: Ten years. I was with The Pretty Things for about four
years . . . I started with the Floyd six months before
Dave Gilmour.

Frank: What does your job involve ?

Pete: Well . . . I'm mainly into sound, so I have to get
together all their sound equipment. A lot of it I've built
myself. I sort of ran around and picked people's brains and
put stuff together, the best I could. Also when we're on the
road, I make sure everything they want is together, like the
stage is right and the power is right, and so on . . . Like
when we did a twelve day tour I had to go around five days
before hand and go to each one of those places we're going
to play in, and just spend the day there talking to the
promoter, the hall manager, and all the electrical heads of
departments, going over our rider and all the things that we
specify, making sure that they're all organised.

Frank: What happens on a typical touring day ?

Pete: The trucks usually hit the hall about ten in the
morning and we catch a plane to meet the trucks and then it
takes all day from ten to four to set the equipment up, at
least ! So the whole day is just spent making sure all the
equipment is working and the band usually come in about
four for a sound check.

Frank: What is the structure of their sound system ?

Pete: On stage Rick's keyboards and stack, Dave's guitar
stack, Nick's drums and Roger's bass gear. At this moment

Hipgnosis

they just use that as a sort of on stage sound which is all carefully miked; and we've got a P.A. and a mixing console which we have in the audience, and also a quadrophonic set up around the house . . .

Frank: Is the quad directly connected to the Floyd?

Pete: The quad system is in addition to the P.A. and is set up behind the stage. at the back of the hall and to the right and left, so the people sitting in the centre round about the mixer get a quadrophonic picture of the sound, like for the tape effects. Also on the mixer you can punch in, say Dave's guitar solo into quad, and pan it around on a joystick and send it round and round the hall – like when Roger does that scream in "Careful With That Axe" you can sort of fade it into quad and have it bombard you from all sides.

Frank: Is the P.A. a specific set of equipment?

Pete: Our P.A. isn't something you can just go in a shop and say "I wanna buy a P.A., John" and come out with that. Our P.A. has developed with the Floyd the way their music's developed.

It's just basically amplifiers, speakers, horn units and high pressure units that we all put together – what I'm trying to do is reproduce the sound that you get at home with a good hi-fi system in the hall, right, with the mixer so you can have complete control of the sound they're making on stage . . . The mikes, which are standard, on stage, they all come up a multicore cable to the mixer and that piece of equipment is specially made for the Floyd – they said what was needed; we had an ordinary mixer but after a few years I chopped it all up and rebuilt it.

Frank: What is the P.A.'s amplification? (Shows me a photo.)

Pete: That's half the amplifiers we use on the P.A. – that's 6 Phase Linear 700s, right, an electronic cross over, and a compressor and we use all that each side of the stage to drive the main P.A. At the mixer we use 4 Phase Linear 400s and 2 Phase Linear 700s to drive the quad system.

Frank: What about their personal stacks?

Pete: Dave plays through a couple of Hi Watt 100s that drive an ordinary traditional 4 x 12 speaker which is essentially just a "monitor" for him on stage, although in fact Dave plays very loud. His main power comes through the P.A. as it does for the others. Roger has 2 x 100 Hi Watt amps driving 2 bass reflex speakers the same as in P.A.

Hipgnosis

and two high frequency horn units on the top.
All Rick's keyboards go through another mixer which he
also sends through either his stack, essentially a monitor,
and is miked through the P.A., or through his Leslies. Nick
doesn't have a monitor because he plays loud enough for
himself and the others to hear.
Frank: And the mixer ?
Pete: Sound travels up the multicore cable plugged into
the back of the mixer and it comes up on a fader like in a
recording studio, and you can equalize the sound that
comes through the microphones and make it treble, bass or
whatever ; you can also have echo, and control the volume
through the P.A. i.e. you do all the instruments on different
faders – like Nick's drum kit, there are ten different mikes
and you set the drum balance and send the whole thing
through another fader, and the vocals are the same,
another sub group. In effect you've got someone sitting in
front of this giant stereo just doing a mix of the band live.
The guy who does it is the guy who did their last album –
instead of doing it bit by bit as in a studio he does it ''live''.
Frank: What speakers do you have for the P.A. ?
Pete: On each side we are using nine bass bins for
reproducing any bass sound between forty cycles to about
eight hundred. Then we've got thirty horn units both sides
some of which are mid range and some are higher range.
I've put these units together using a number of makes –
Electrovoice equipment (bass range) JBL equipment
(treble range) Vitavox equipment (mid range) – They're
just brand components which I've used and put together
for what I think is the best hi-fi.
Frank: So, the sound travels from . . .
Pete: All the mikes pick up the signal and send it down the
multicore on a balanced line to be amplified by the mixer
which is like a giant pre-amp – then you send it out on faders
down another multicore which is a stage return which then
goes to an electronic cross over unit which splits the signal
three ways and sends it to the brass section of amplifiers,
and the treble section and the mid range section of
amplifiers. From the amplifiers they go three ways right to
the bass units, the treble units and the mid range units.
It's all split up and goes to the different sections.
Frank: This for every single bit of sound put out by the
band and from tapes ?

Jill Furmanovsky

Pete: Yeah!

Frank: Is that why it's so clear?

Pete: Well . . . yes . . . but it's just part of a lot of things put together over the years . . . trying to get all parts better, trying, in effect to get a studio effect in a hall!

Later on two further points were made clear :-

1. The cross over system ensures that the right sound (bass, treble or mid range) goes to the right speaker. Thus each speaker is used efficiently and does not try to reproduce sounds for which it is not specifically equipped.

2. The nearer you are to the maximum noise output the more you are likely to distort (just try turning your amp or player full on). The Floyd have enough amplification not to have to "overload" their speakers even at their loudest.

Pete assessed his role in the Floyd as reproducing to the very best of his ability the sounds that the band want in a way that can reach a large audience. I feel that it may be more than this. His contribution to the sound apparatus is a necessary part of Floyd music. The way the music is reproduced has itself an influence on the subsequent writing and desired "quality" of the sound job.

Somebody else could do his job, but then perhaps Floyd music wouldn't sound as it does.

Road Crew

Peter Watts: Road Manager

Arthur Max: Lighting and effects

Graeme Fleming: Lighting Technician

Paul Padun: Lighting Technician – on tour only

Chris Adamson: Sets up and maintains stage equipment

Mick 'The Pole' Kluczynski: General Factotum, Tape Operator, Drum Kit, Quad

Alan Parsons: On tour mixer – Recording Engineer for albums

Robbie Williams: Stage Crew

Bobby Richardson: Stage Crew

On Tour: Trucking Crew – Four drivers and two forty-foot Trailer Tractors

At Gig: 2 fork lift drivers, 6 stage hands, 2 electricians, 2 soundmen, 8 follow spot operators, 1 house electrician

LEGEND OF MUSICAL SYMBOLS

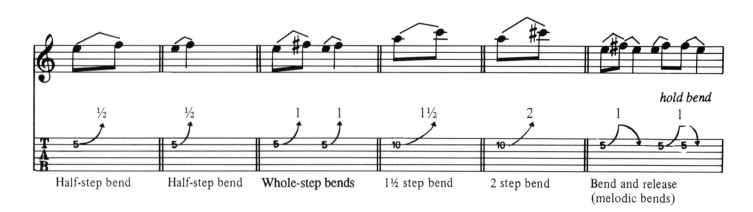

Half-step bend | Half-step bend | **Whole-step bends** | 1½ step bend | 2 step bend | Bend and release (melodic bends)

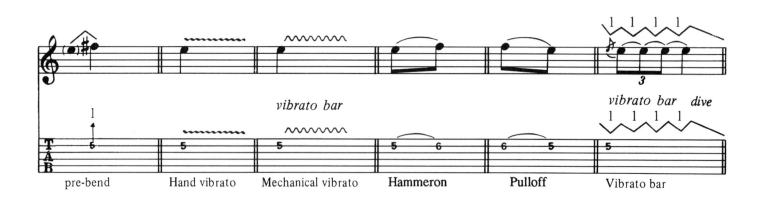

pre-bend | Hand vibrato | Mechanical vibrato | **Hammeron** | **Pulloff** | Vibrato bar

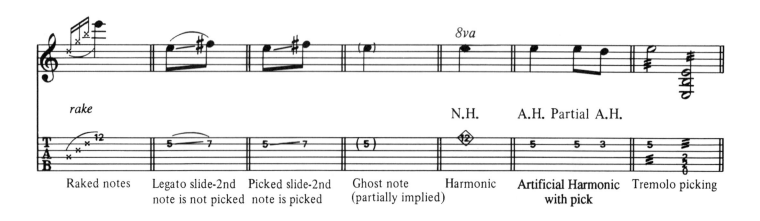

Raked notes | Legato slide-2nd note is not picked | Picked slide-2nd note is picked | Ghost note (partially implied) | Harmonic | **Artificial Harmonic with pick** | Tremolo picking

Palm muting | **Stacatto phrasing** | Unpitched, percussive notes. | Unison bend | **Microtonal bends** (¼ and ¾ step) | Right-hand tapping

BREATHE

Words by
ROGER WATERS

Music by
ROGER WATERS,
DAVID GILMOUR & RICK WRIGHT

Moderately fast with half time feel ♩ = 126

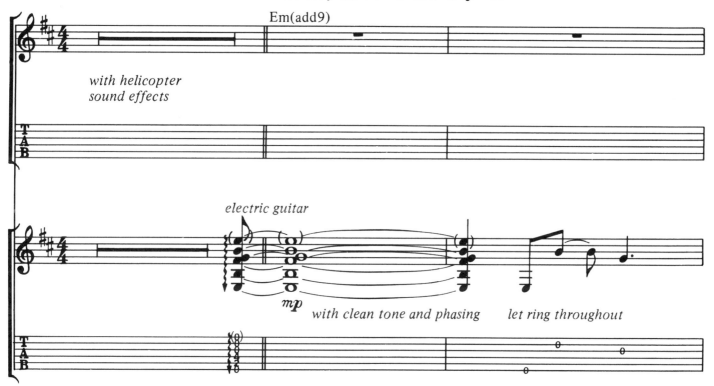

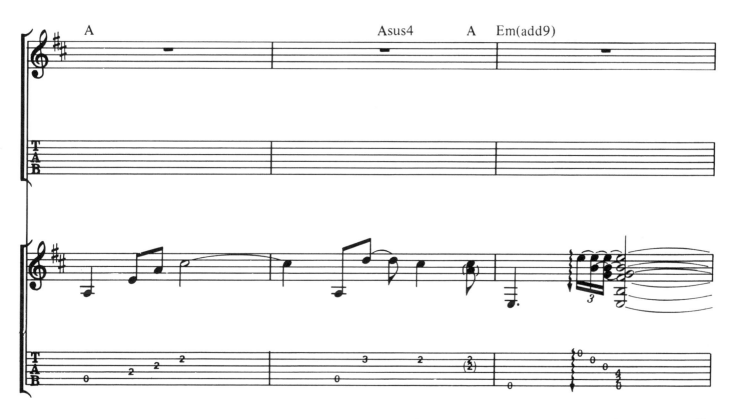

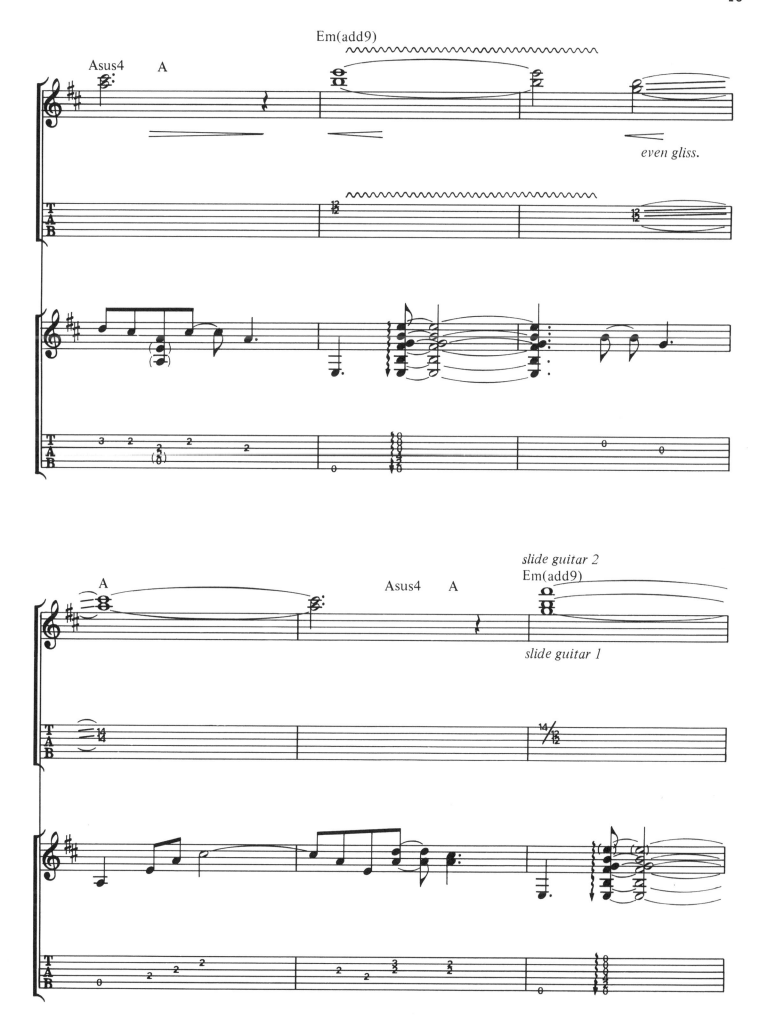

even gliss.

slide guitar 1
Em(add9)

even gliss.

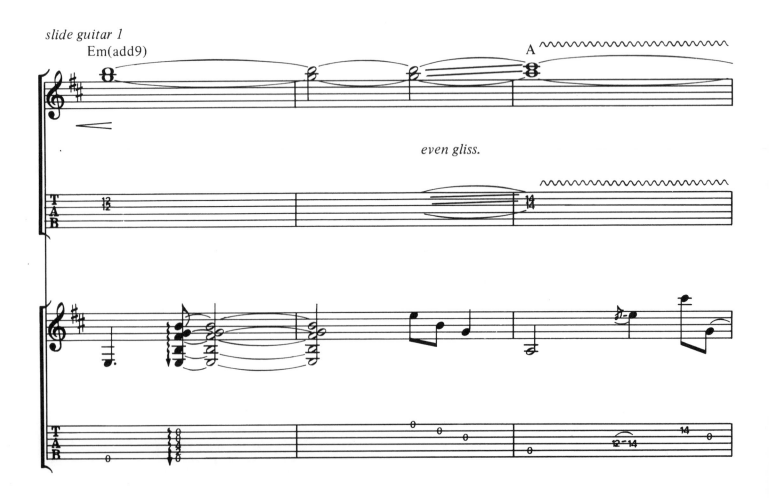

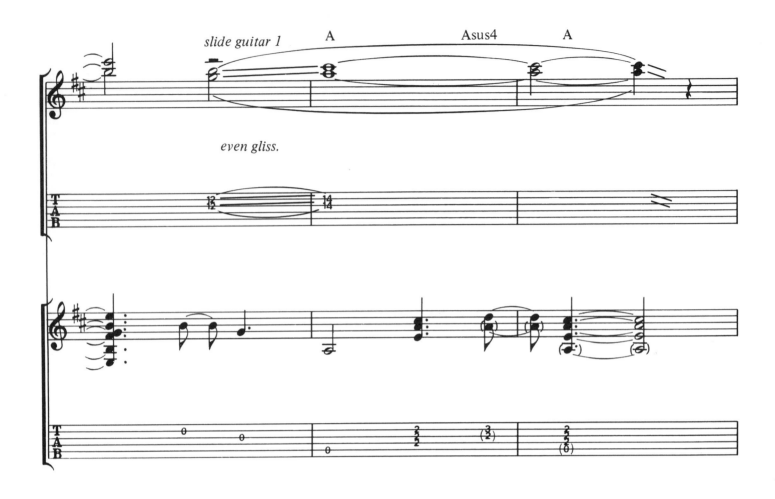

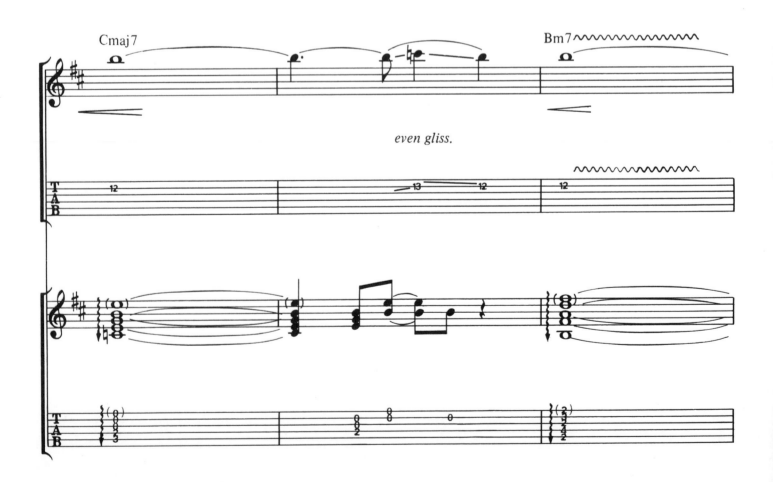

Choose your own___ ground.   For

even gliss.   *even gliss.*

long   you live,___ And high you fly,   And smiles you'll give,___ And tears___

even gliss.

28

When,___ at last,___ the work___ is

even gliss.

done,___

Don't___ sit down,___ it's time___

30

TRUCKING WITH THE FLOYD

TIME

Words by
ROGER WATERS

Music by
DAVID GILMOUR, RICK WRIGHT,
NICK MASON & ROGER WATERS

Moderately with half time feel ♩ = 128

Intro
electric guitar 1

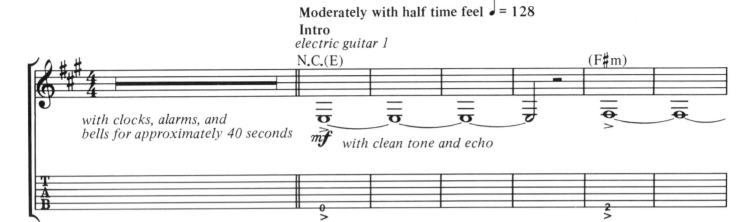

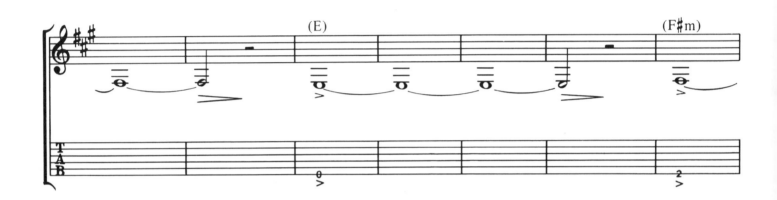

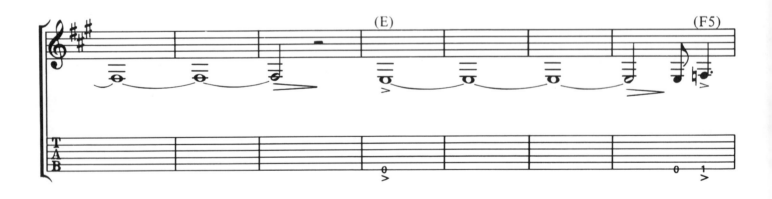

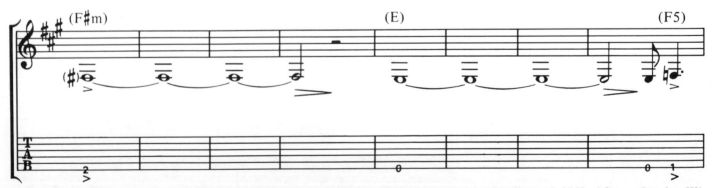

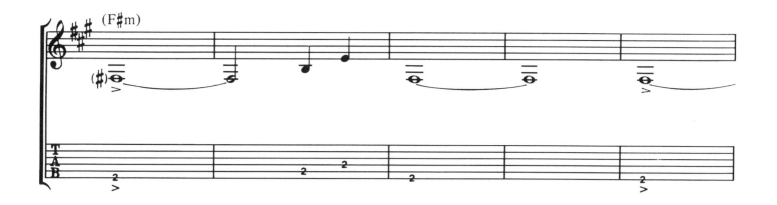

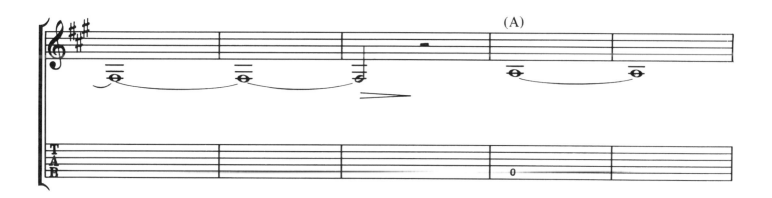

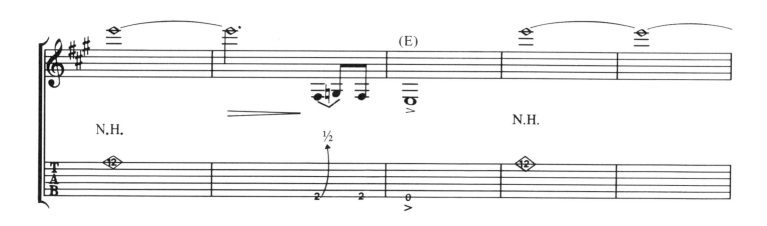

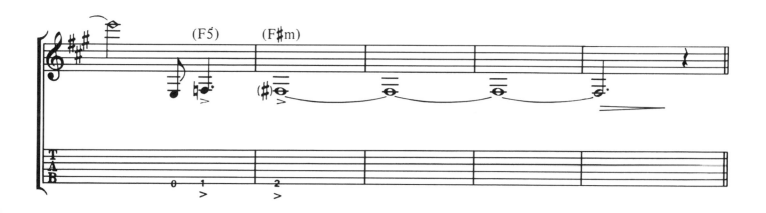

piece of ground__ in your home town.__

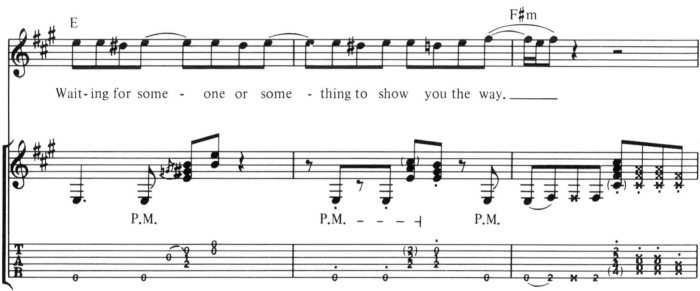

Wait-ing for some - one or some - thing to show you the way._____

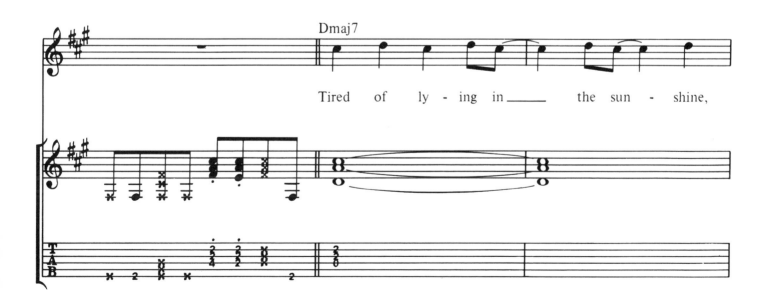

Tired of ly - ing in_____ the sun - shine,

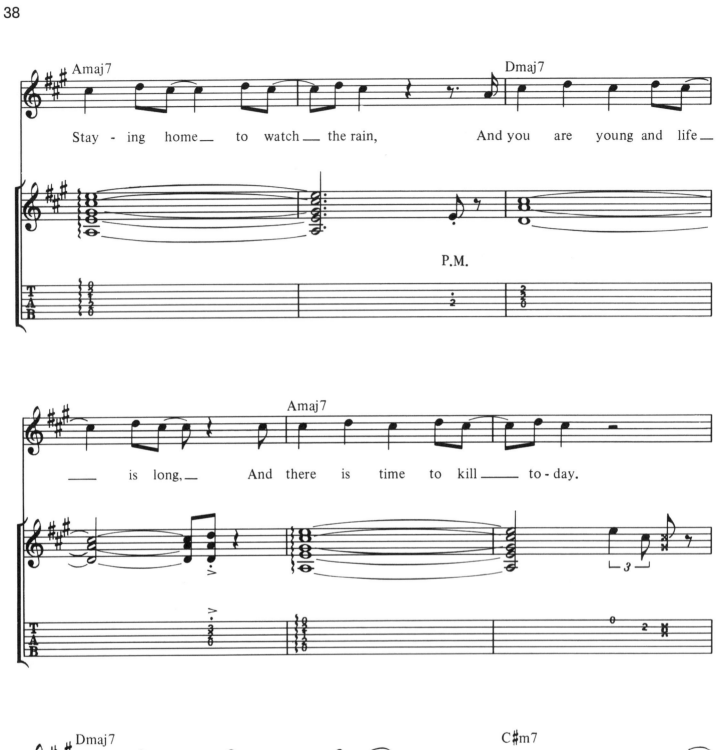

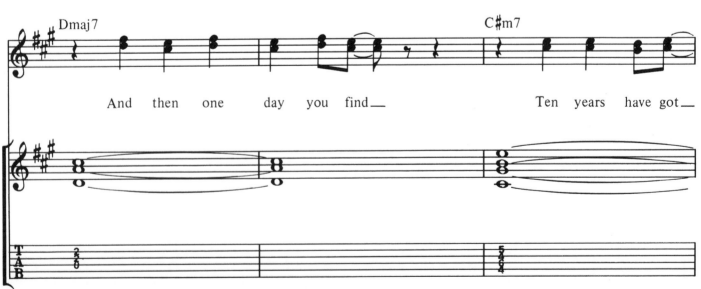

even release

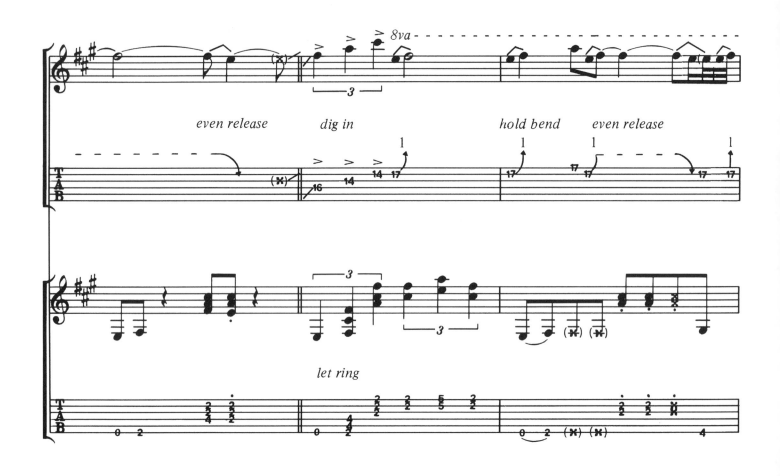

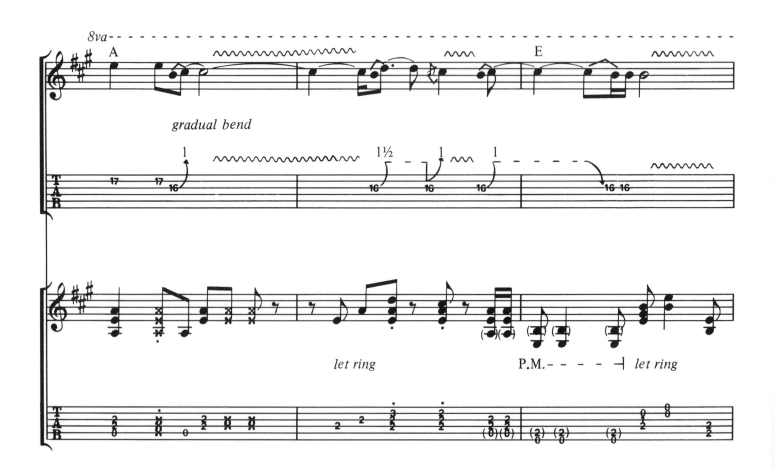

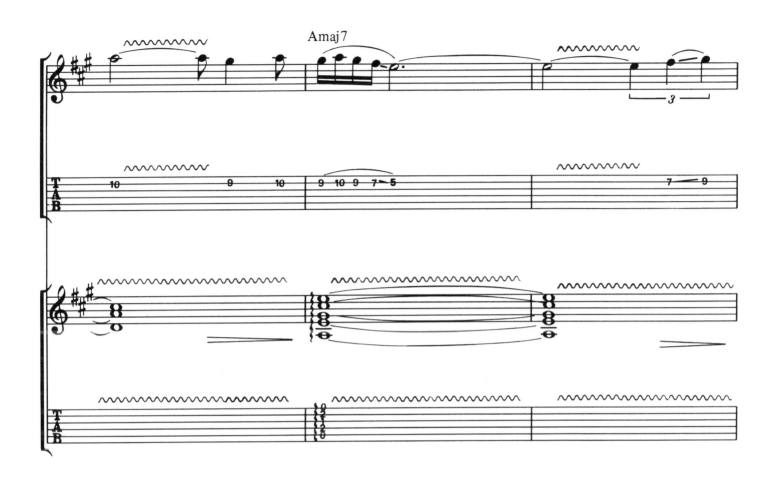

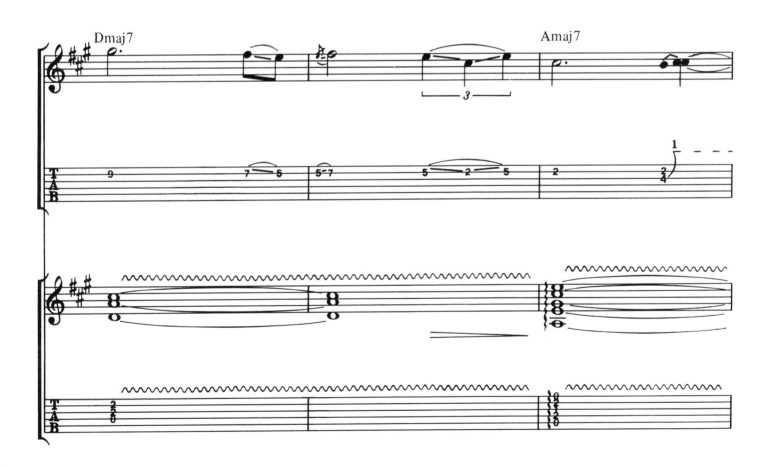

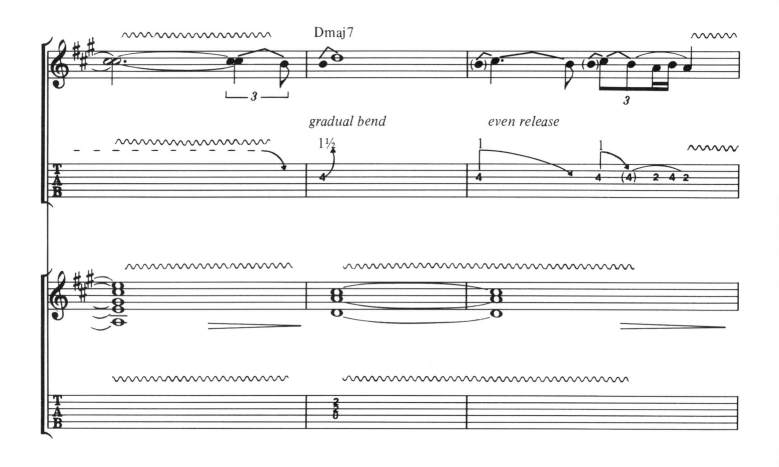

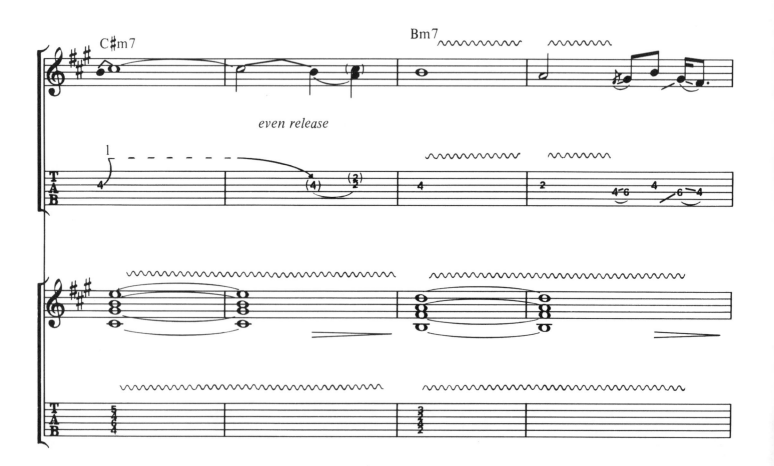

- ing. ___

Rac - ing a - round ___ to come up be - hind ___ you a - gain. ___

The

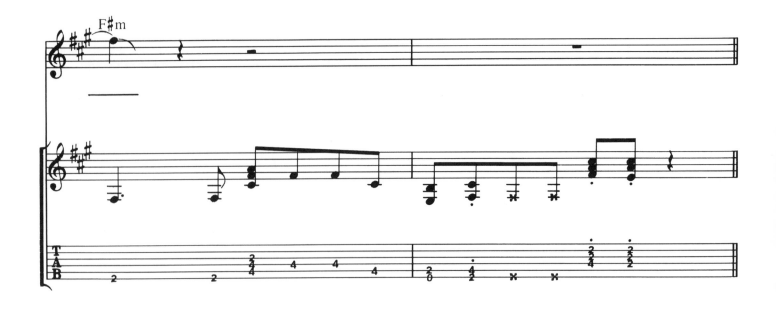

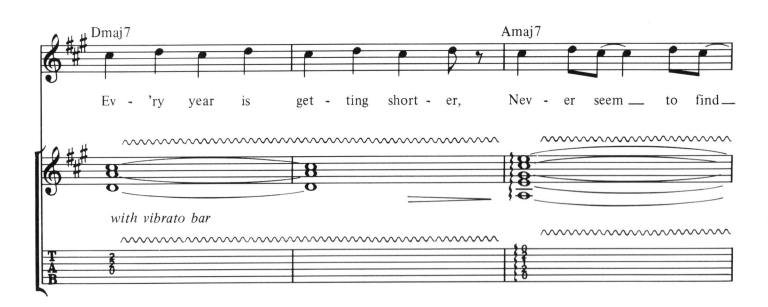

Ev - 'ry year is get - ting short - er, Nev - er seem __ to find __

with vibrato bar

__ the time. __ Plans that ei - ther come __ to naught, Or

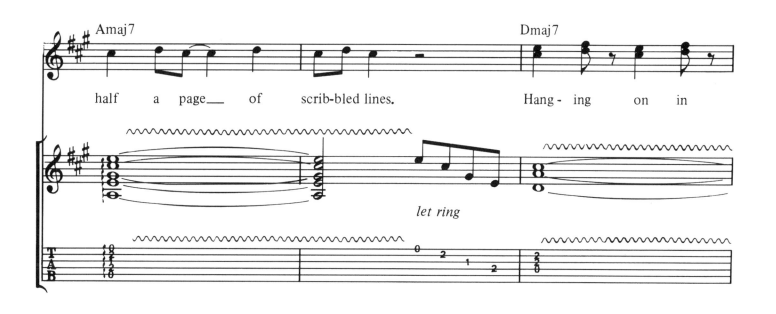

half a page__ of scrib-bled lines. Hang - ing on in

let ring

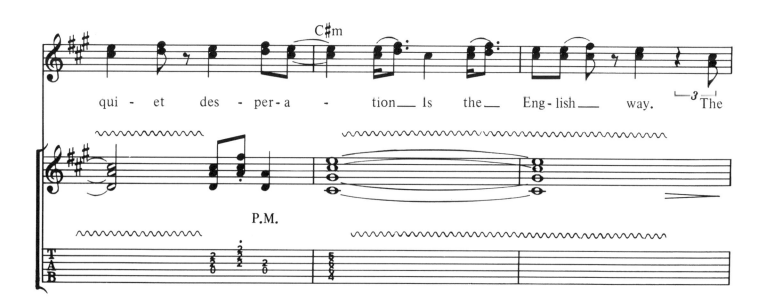

qui - et des - per - a - tion__ Is the__ Eng - lish__ way. The

P.M.

Segue to "Breathe (Reprise)"

time is gone,__ the song is o - ver. Thought I'd some-thing more to say.__

mf

BREATHE (Reprise)

Words by
ROGER WATERS

Music by
ROGER WATERS,
DAVID GILMOUR & RICK WRIGHT

Moderately with half time feel ♩ = 122

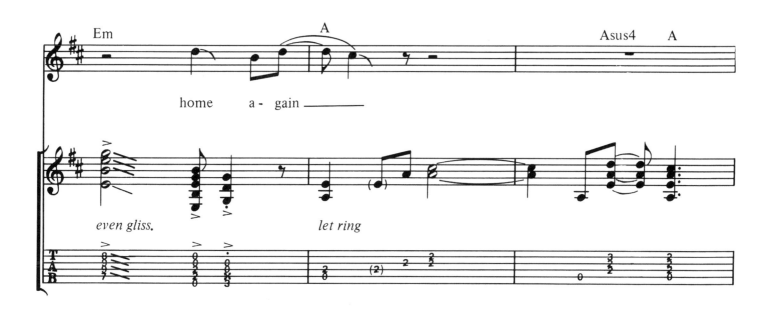

home a - gain ____

even gliss.   *let ring*

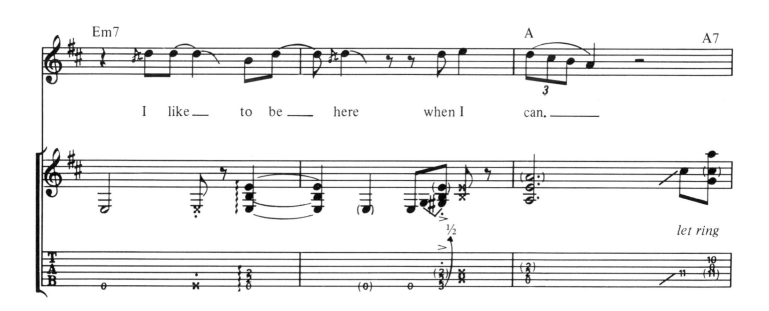

I like ____ to be ____ here   when I   can. ____

let ring

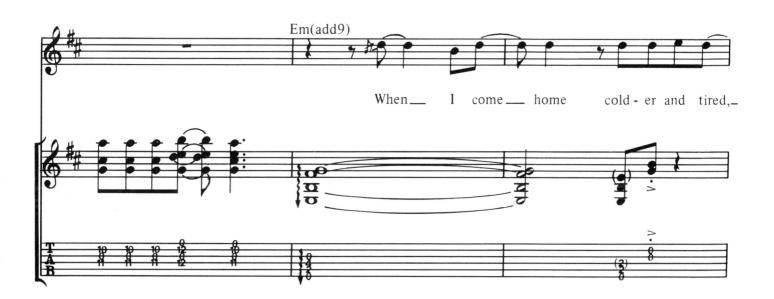

When ____ I come ____ home   cold - er and tired, ____

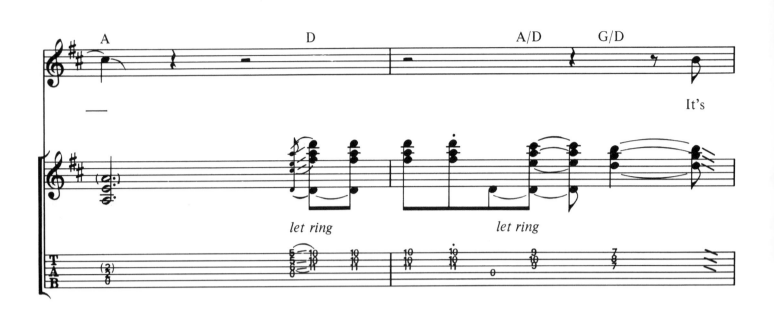

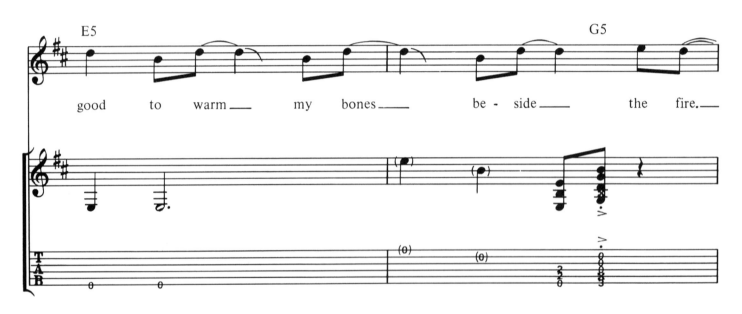

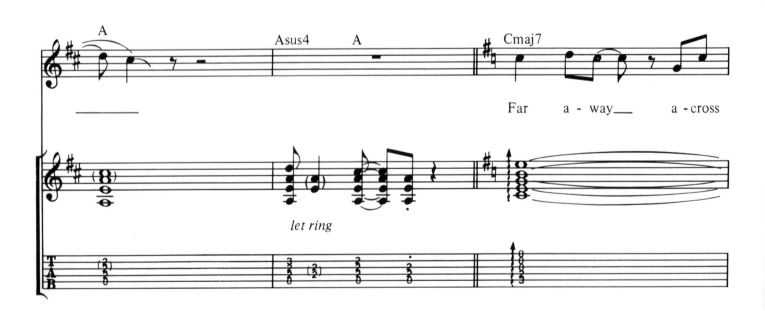

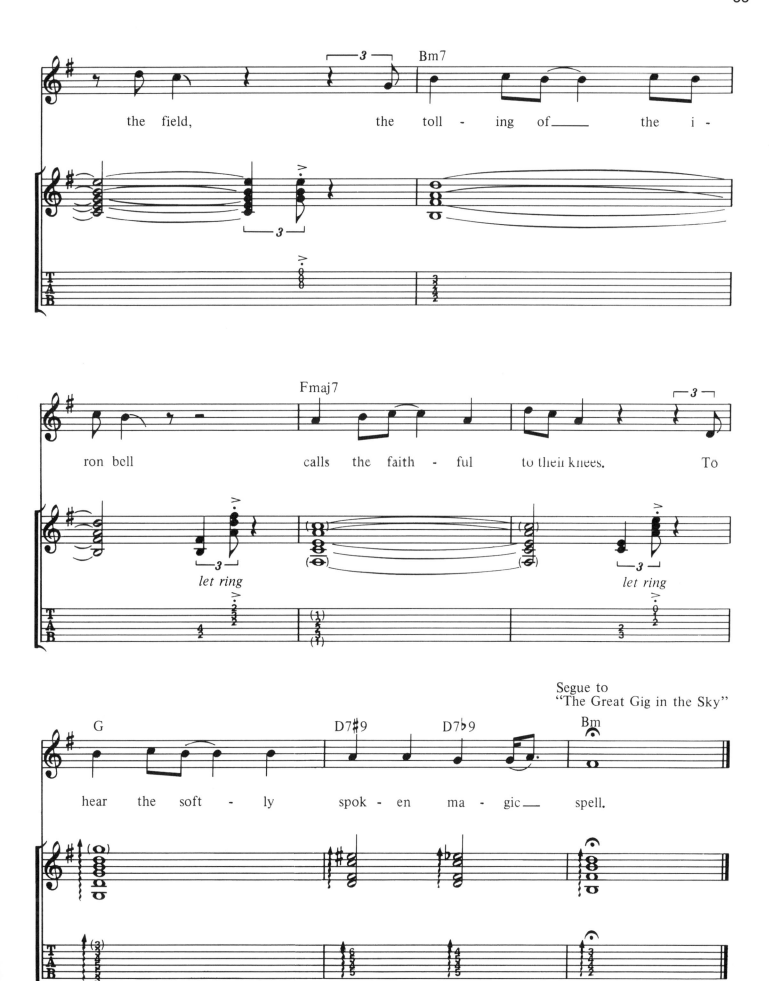

the field,   the toll - ing of____ the i -

ron bell   calls the faith - ful to their knees.   To

hear the soft - ly spok - en ma - gic____ spell.

Segue to
"The Great Gig in the Sky"

THE GREAT GIG IN THE SKY

Music by
RICK WRIGHT

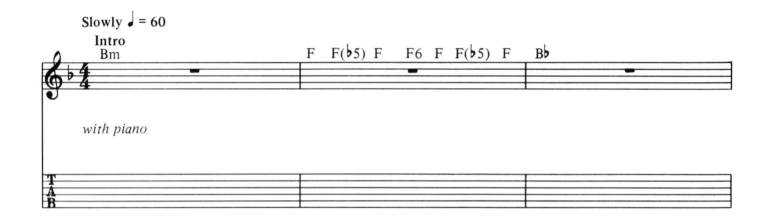

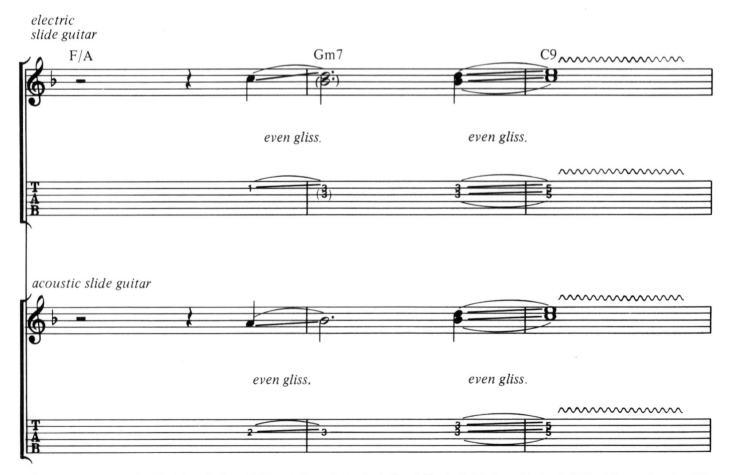

Spoken: "And I am not

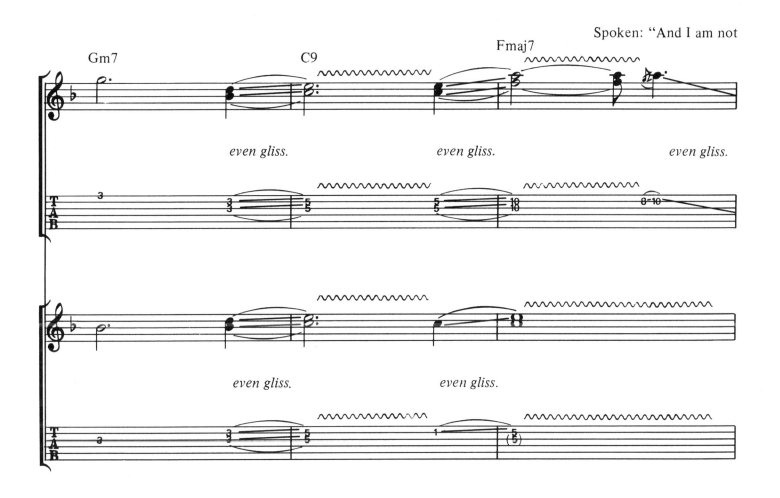

even gliss.

frightened of dying; anytime will do, I don't mind.

Why should I be frightened of dying? There's no reason for it; you're got to go sometime."

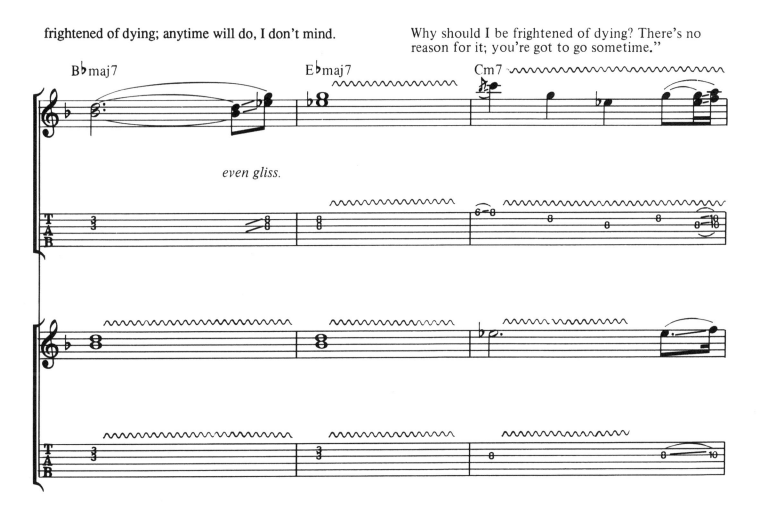

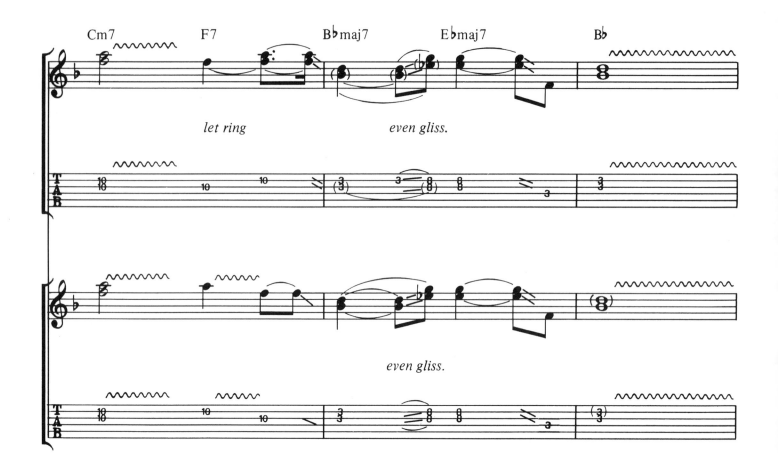

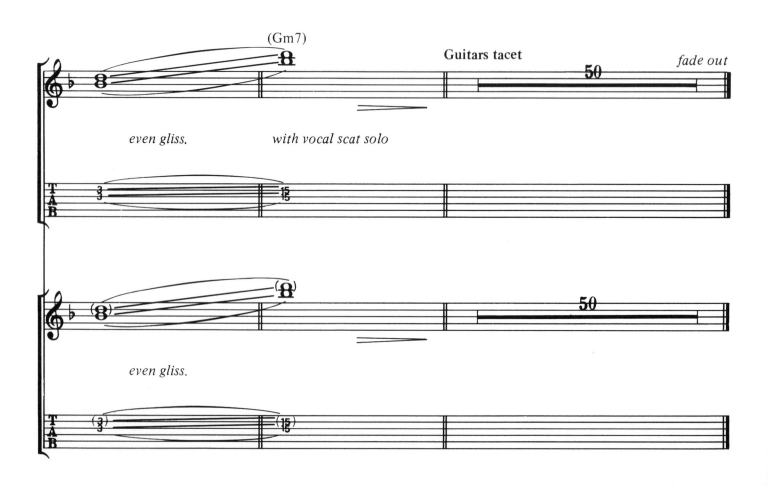

MONEY

Words and Music by
ROGER WATERS

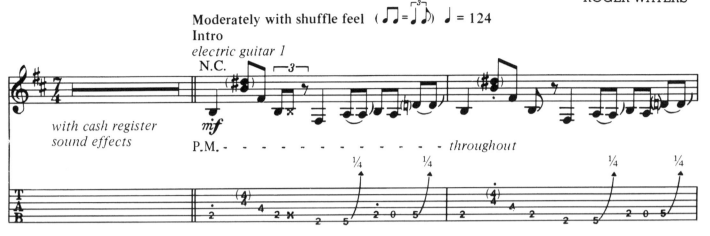

60

Verse 1,2,3

1. Mon-ey, you get a - way. ___ You get a
2. Mon-ey, you get ___ back. ___ I'm ___
3. Mon-ey, it's a crime. ___ Share ___

good   job   with   more pay and you're O._____ K.   Mon-
all   right, Jack, keep your hands off- a my_____ stack.   Mon-
it   fair - ly   but don't take a slice of my_____ pie.   Mon-

ey,_____   it's   a   gas.   Grab,
ey,_____   it's   a   hit.   But don't
ey,_____   so they   say,   Is

think I'll buy me a foot - ball _____ team.
set and I think I need a Lear _____ jet.
prise that they're giv - ing none a -

*Play on Verse 2 only

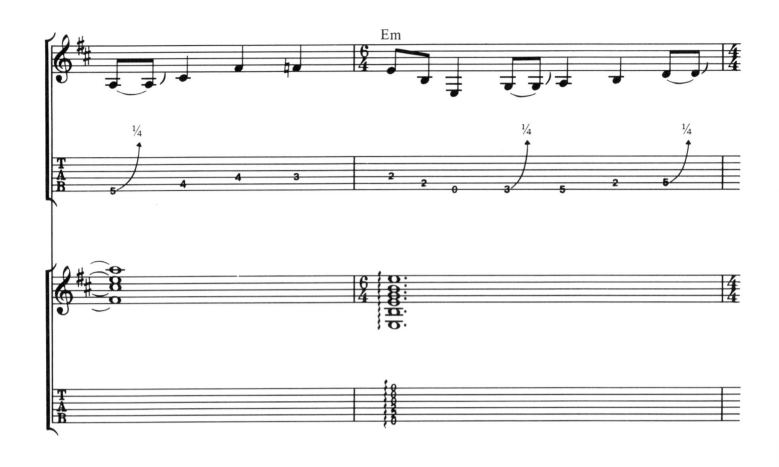

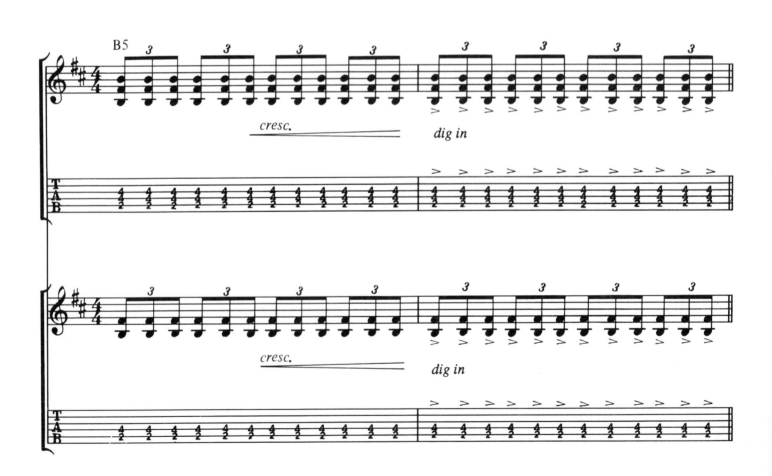

Guitar solo 1

lead guitar 1

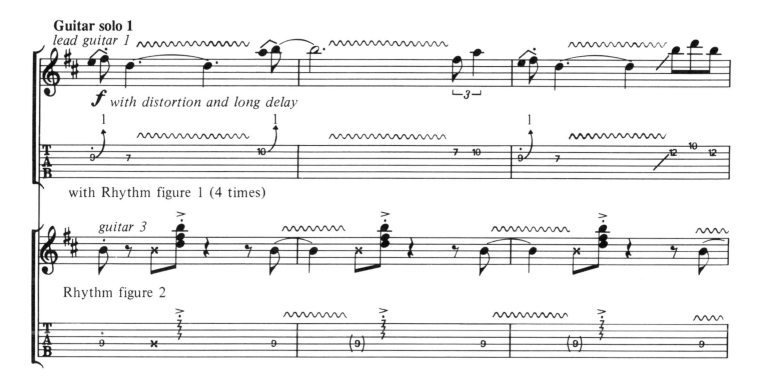

f *with distortion and long delay*

with Rhythm figure 1 (4 times)

guitar 3

Rhythm figure 2

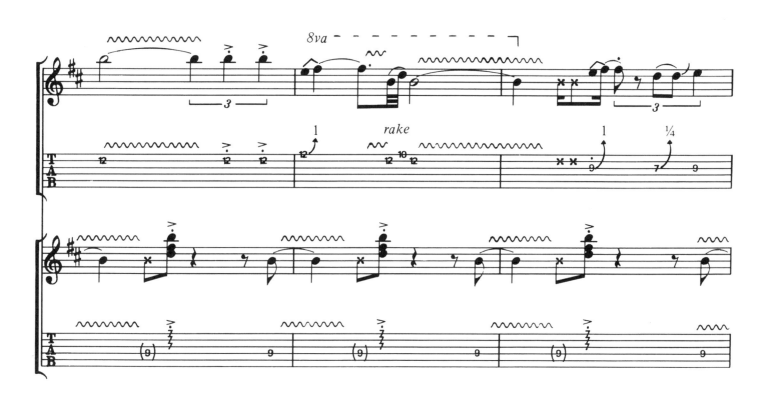

8va

rake

Rhythm figure 1

P.M.

70

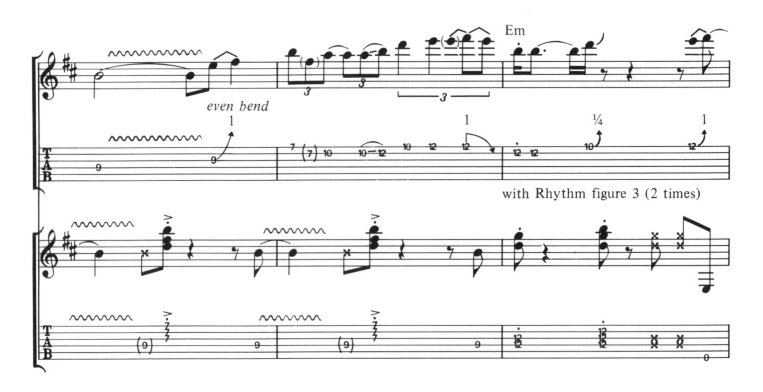

with Rhythm figure 3 (2 times)

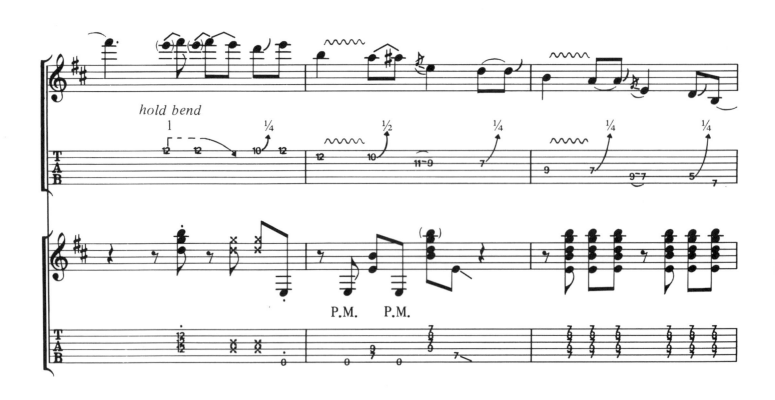

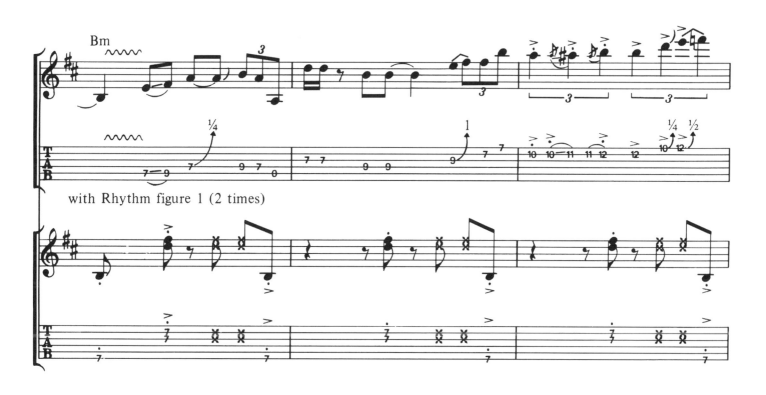

with Rhythm figure 1 (2 times)

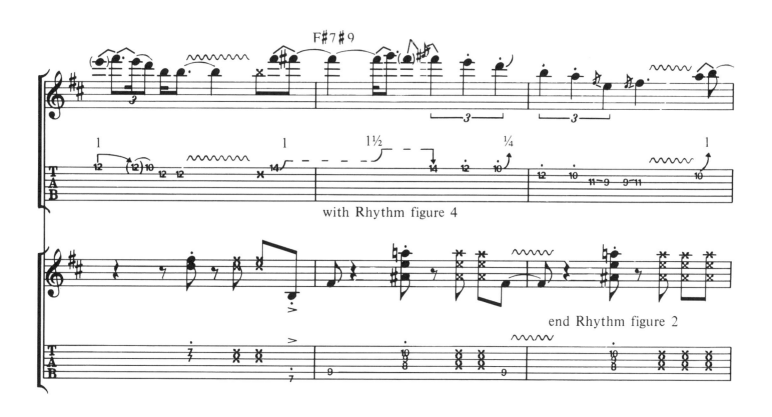

with Rhythm figure 4

end Rhythm figure 2

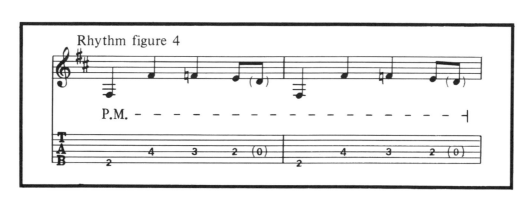

Rhythm figure 4

P.M. - - - - - - - - - - - - - - - - - -

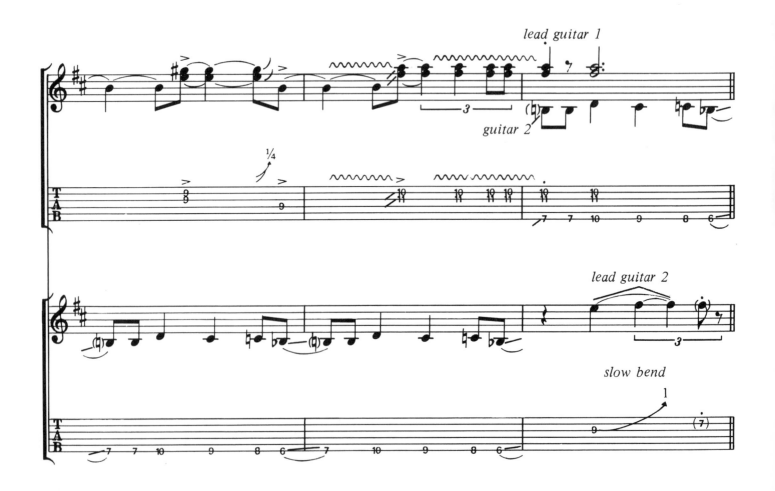

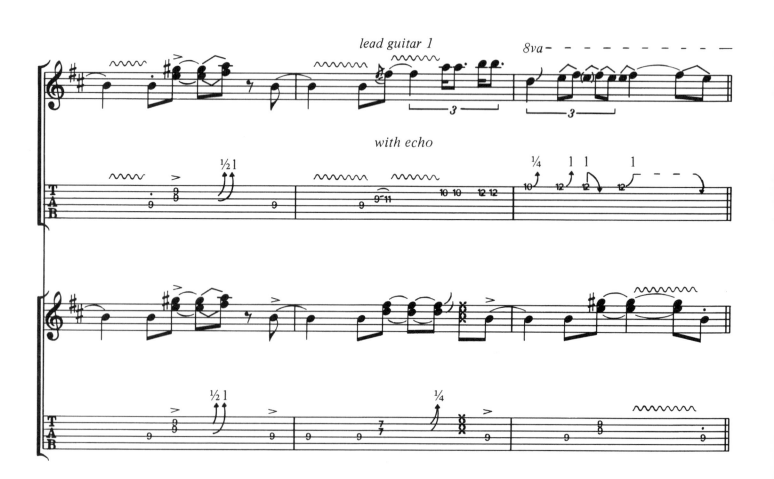

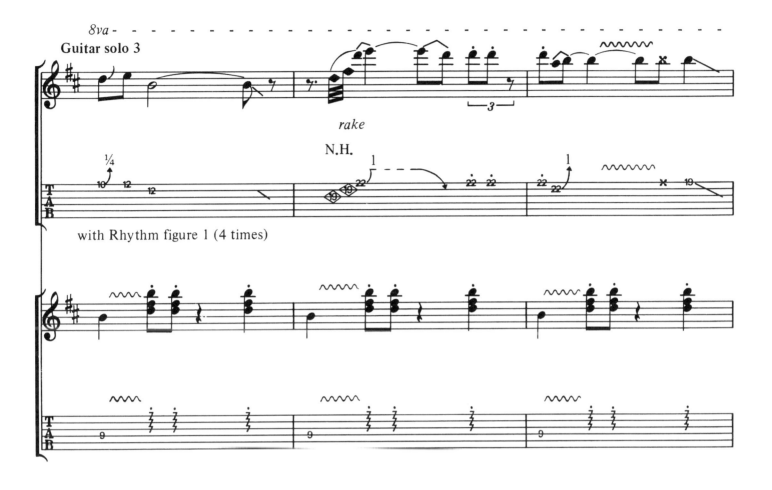

with Rhythm figure 1 (4 times)

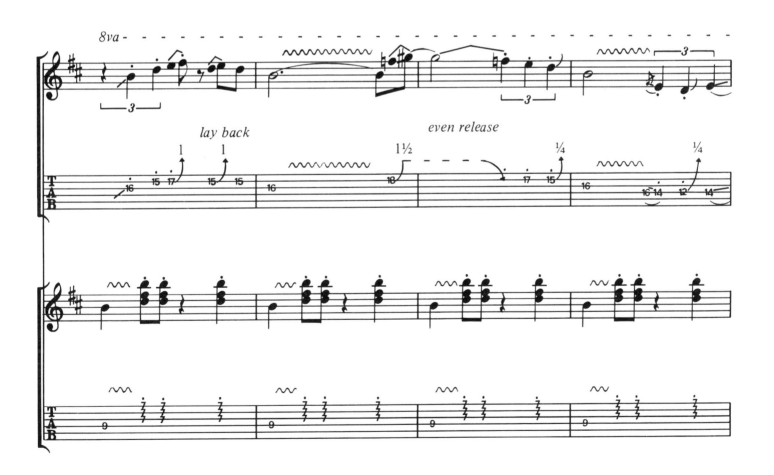

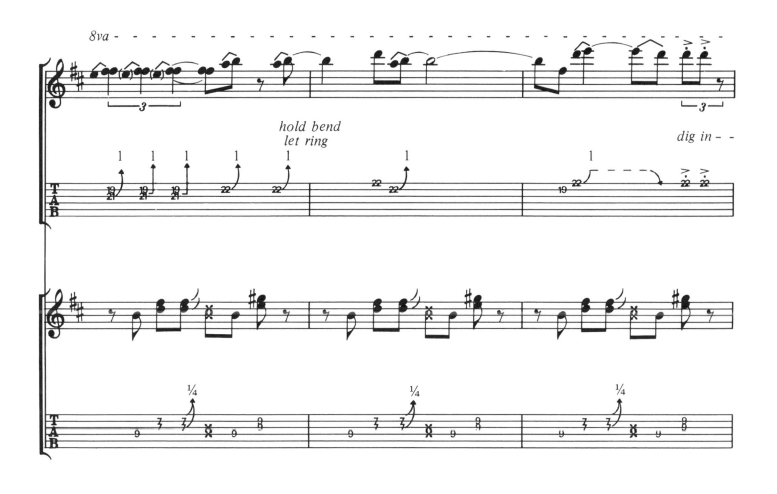

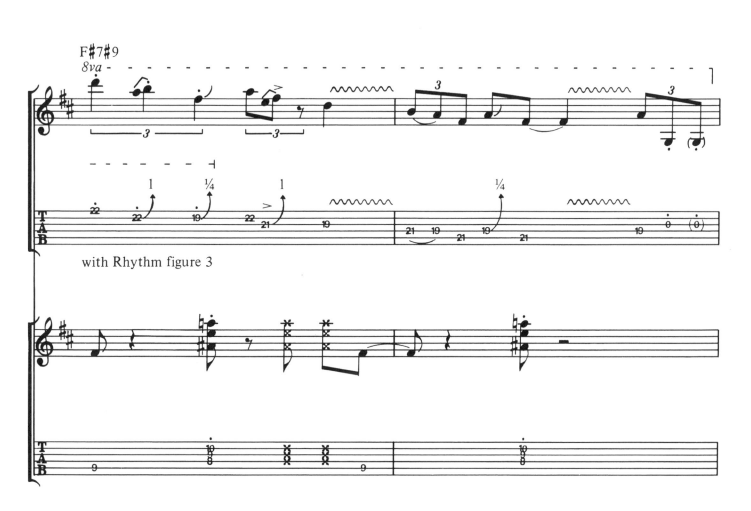

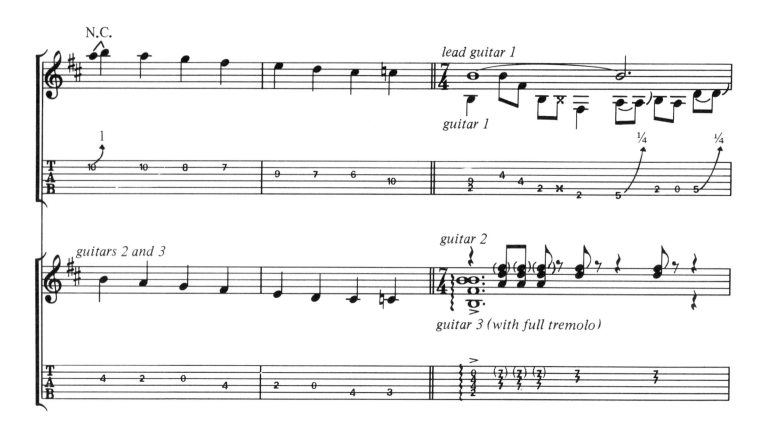

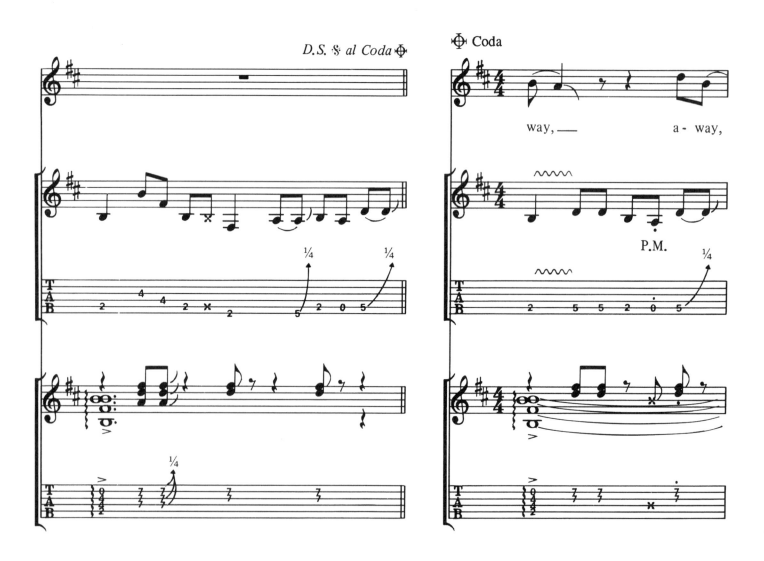

way,_____   Woo!_____

vocal ad lib simile with
background conversation effects

P.M.   P.M.   P.M.

begin fade

P.M.   P.M.   *p*   P.M.

Segue to "Us and Them"

Spoken: *"I don't know;
I was drunk at the time."*

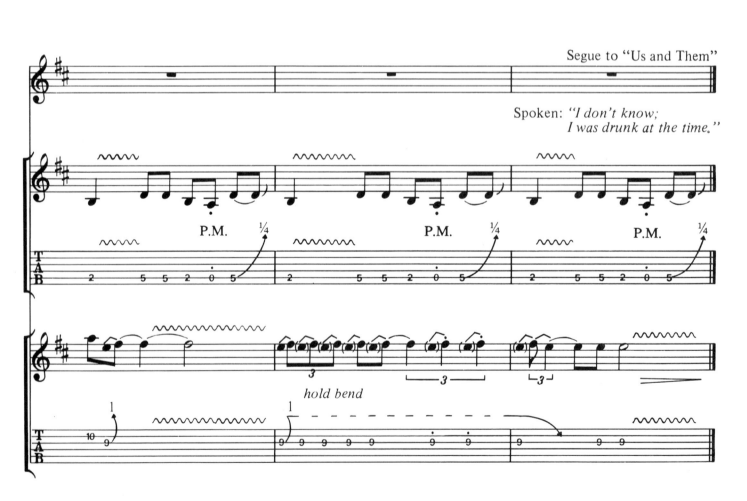

US AND THEM

Words by
ROGER WATERS

Music by
RICK WRIGHT

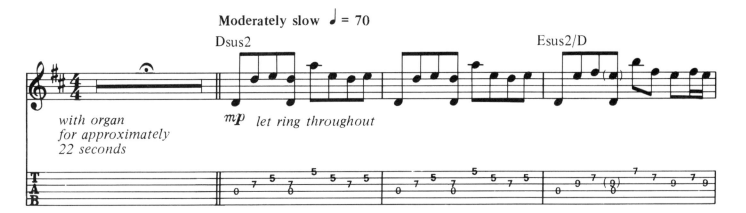

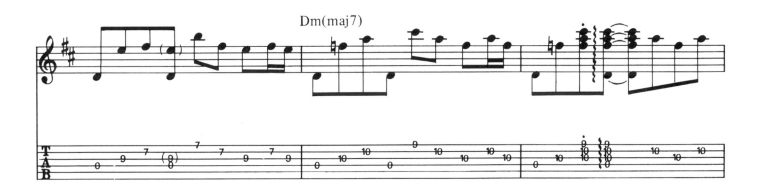

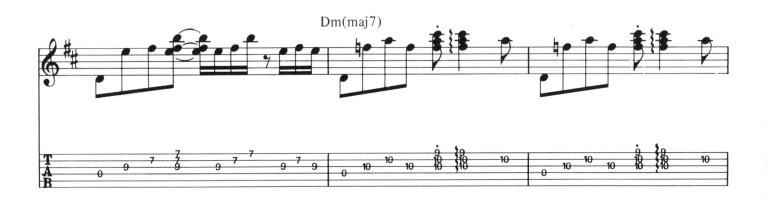

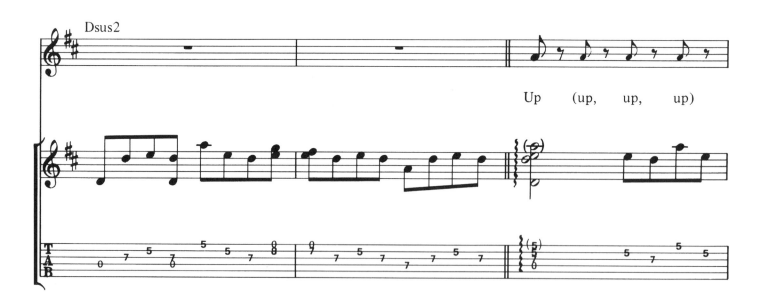

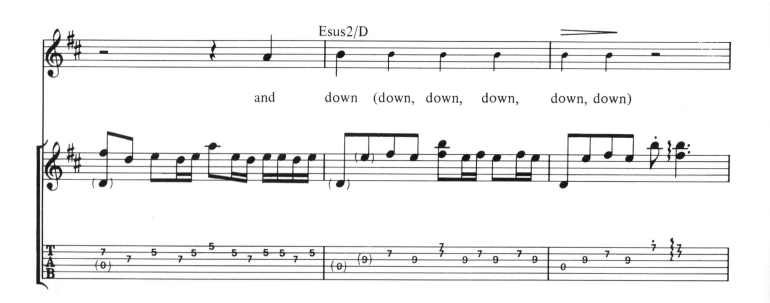

and in the end ___ it's on - ly 'round and 'round ('round, 'round) and

fade in with volume pedal

'round ('round, 'round, 'round)

guitar 1

guitar 2

f *with distortion*

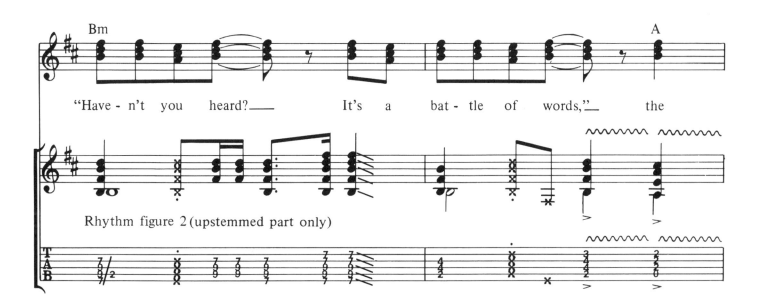

"Have - n't you heard? ___ It's a bat - tle of words," the

Rhythm figure 2 (upstemmed part only)

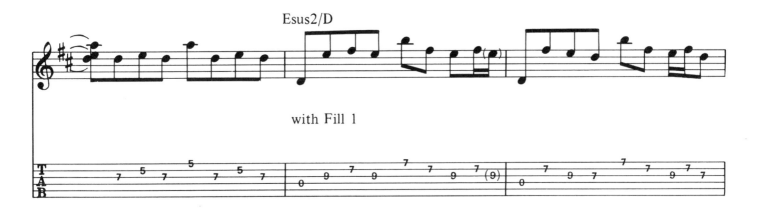

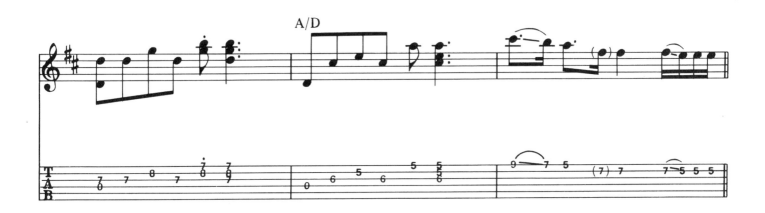

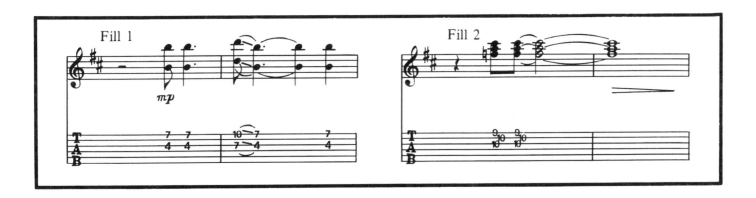

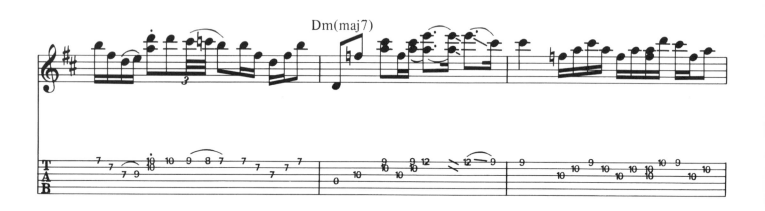

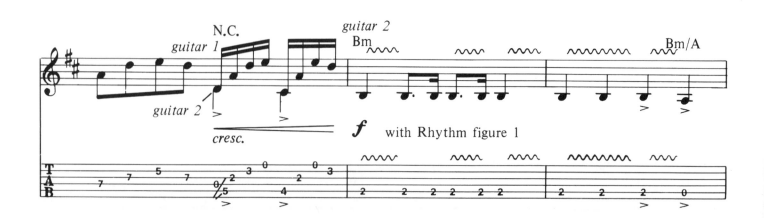

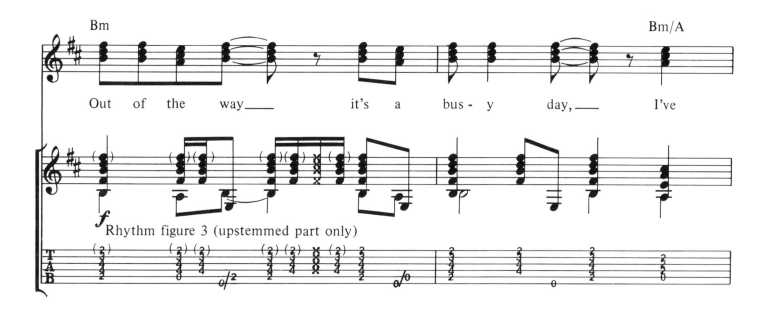

Out of the way___ it's a bus - y day,___ I've

got things on my___ mind. For want of the price___ of

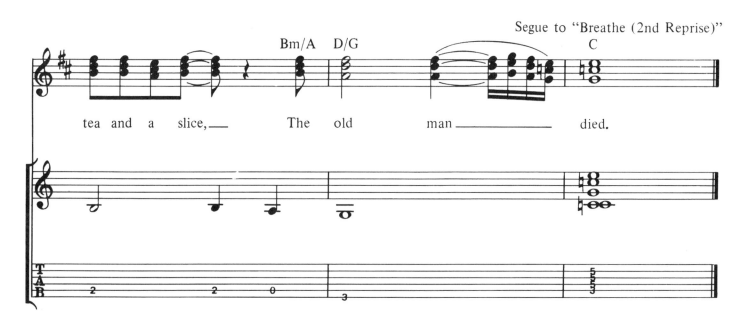

tea and a slice,___ The old man___ died.

BREATHE (Second Reprise)

Words by
ROGER WATERS

Music by
ROGER WATERS,
DAVID GILMOUR & RICK WRIGHT

Moderately slow with half time feel ♩ = 73
Synthesizer solo

Guitar solo (with unison scat singing)

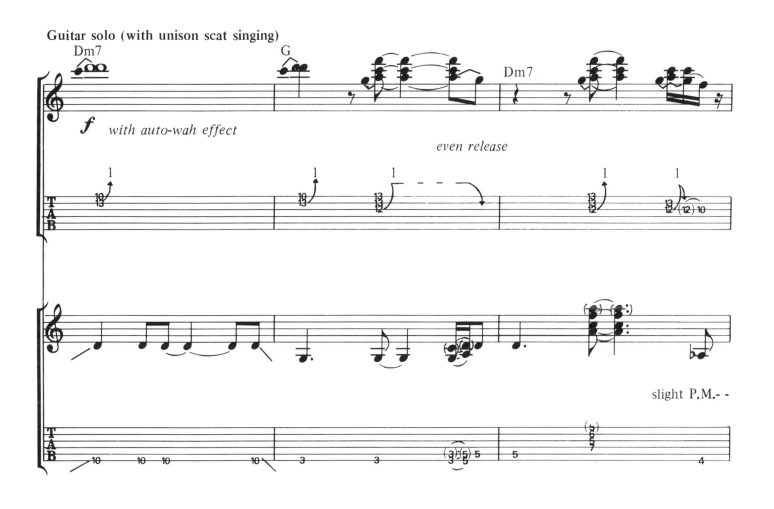

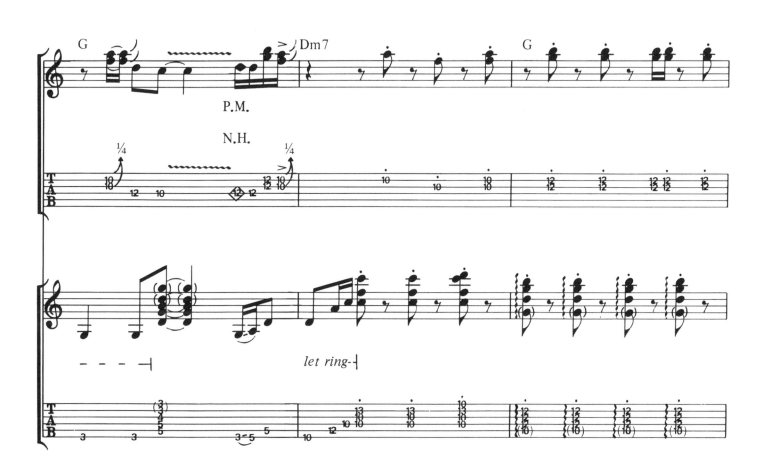

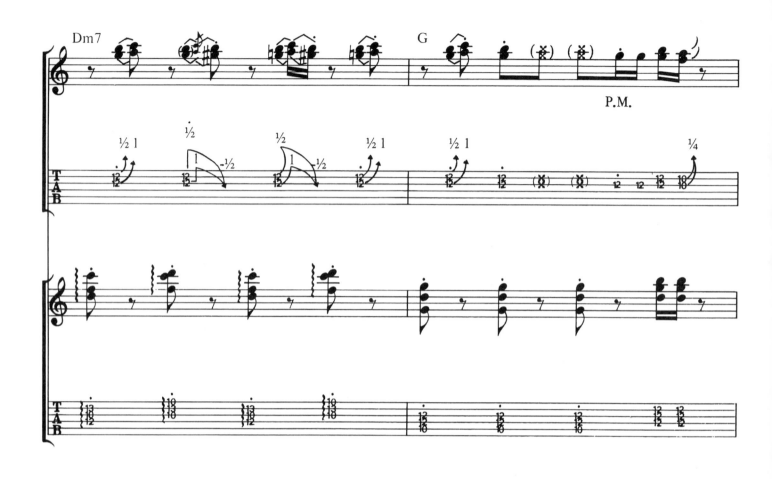

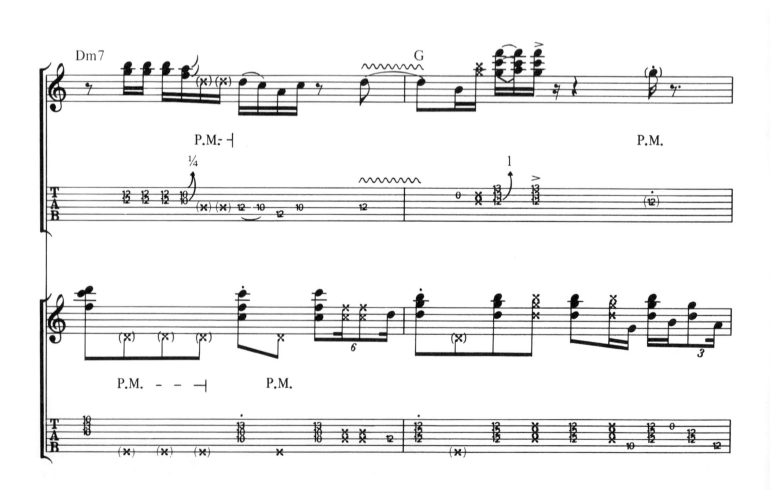

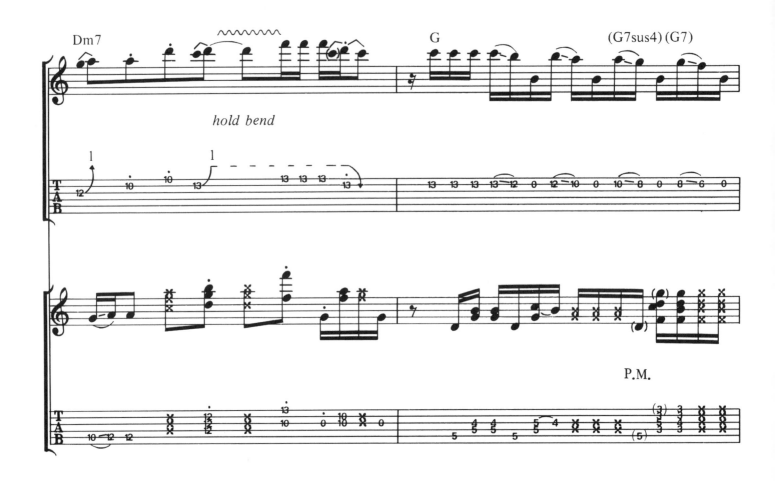

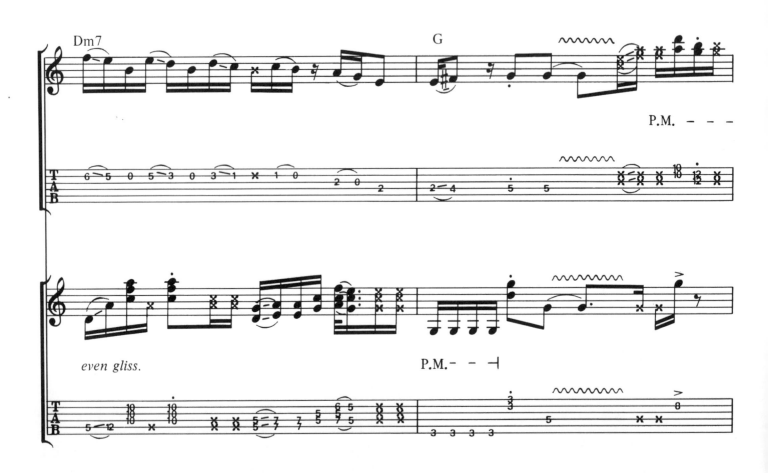

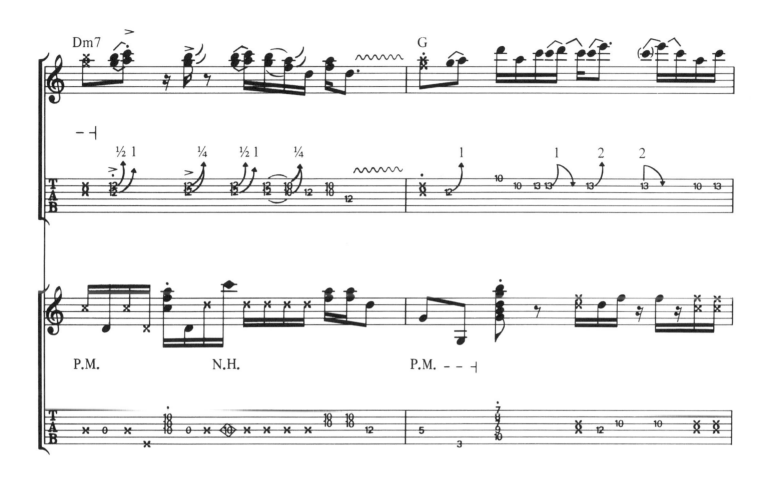

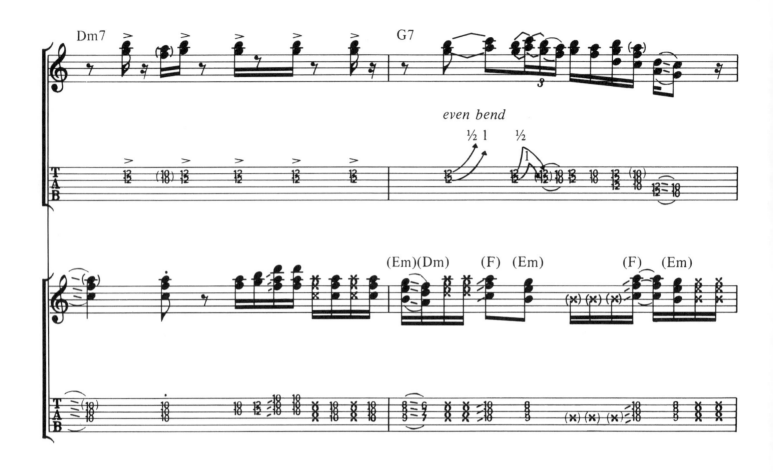

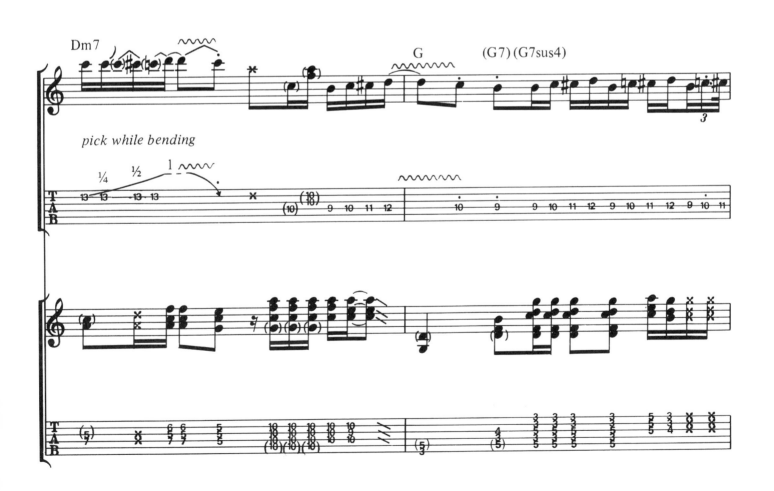

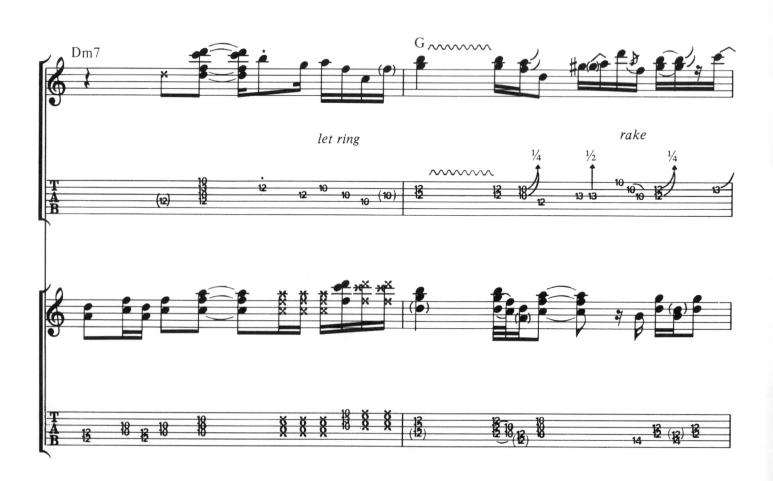

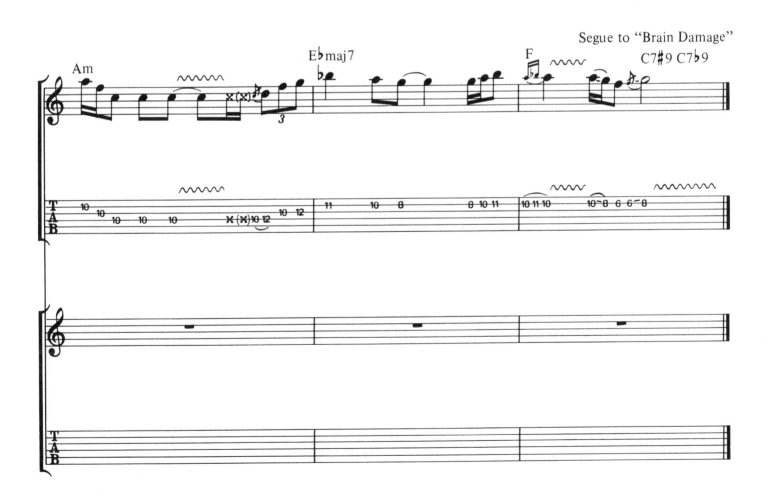

BRAIN DAMAGE

Words and Music by
ROGER WATERS

110

Got to keep the loon - ies on the path.

The lu - na - tic

8va

even gliss.

The lu - na - tic ____ is in my head. __

You raise ___ the blade, __

even gliss.

You make the change,

even gliss.

You re-ar-range me till I'm sane.

head, but it's not me.

And if the cloud bursts thun - der in your ear,

side ___ of the moon. ___   Ah,

Ah, ___   Ah.

ECLIPSE

Words and Music by
ROGER WATERS

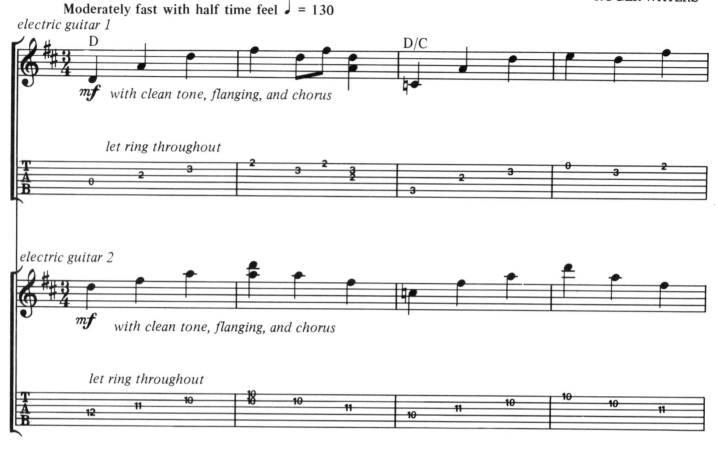

All that you touch, And all that you

see, All that you taste,

All you feel, And all that you

Rhythm figure 1

love, And all that you hate,____

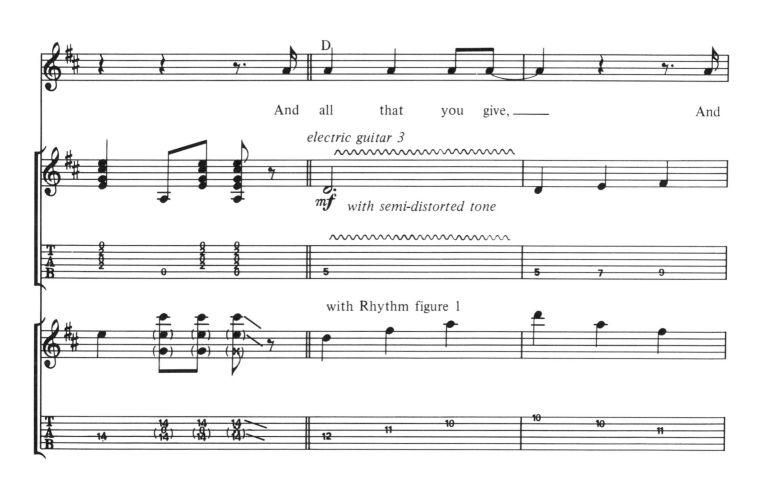

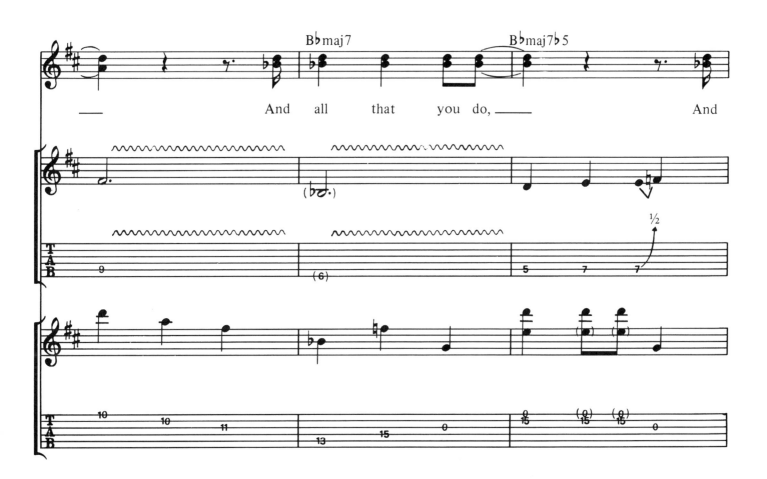

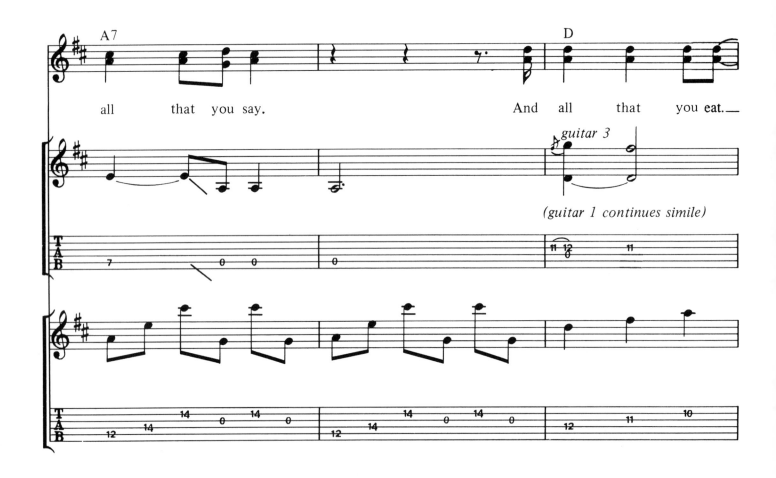

all   that   you say.   And   all   that   you eat.__

guitar 3

(guitar 1 continues simile)

__   And   ev - 'ry   one   you meet,   And

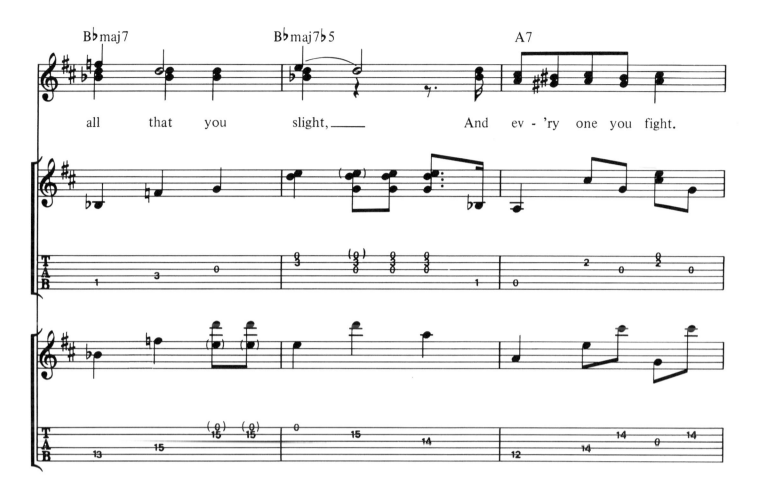

all that you slight,_____ And ev - 'ry one you fight.

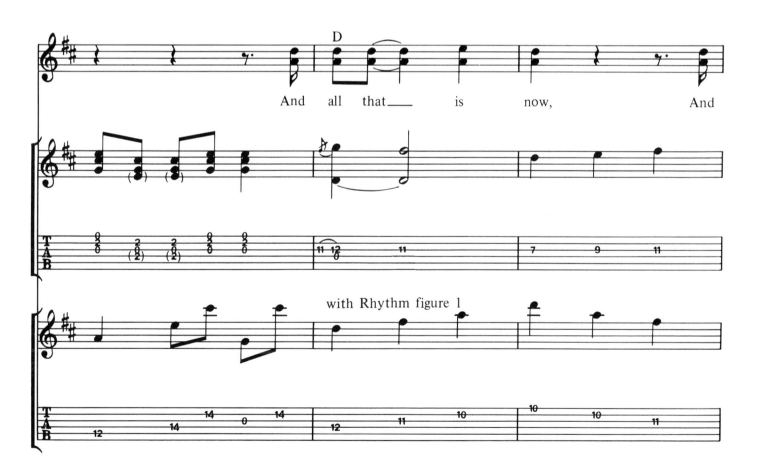

And all that_____ is now, And

all that__ is gone, And all that's to come,__

And ev - 'ry thing__ un - der the__

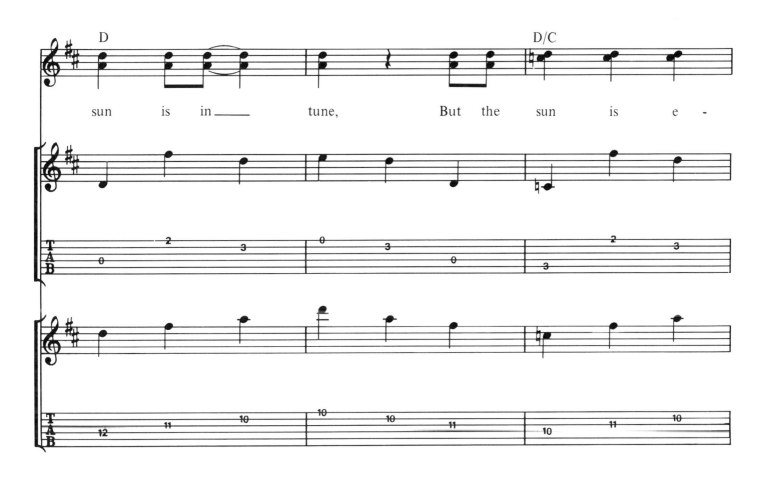

sun   is   in _____   tune,   But   the   sun   is   e -

clipsed   by   the   moon. _____   *with heartbeat effects*

Hipgnosis

Jill Furmanovsky

Robert Failla   Rainbow

Hipgnosis

Hipgnosis

Jill Furmanovsky

Pink Floyd

David Gilmour · Lead Guitar and Vocals
Richard Wright · Keyboards and Vocals
Roger Waters · Bass Guitar and Vocals
Nick Mason · Drums

Album discography

The Piper at the Gates of Dawn
Columbia. SCX 6517. September 1967
Astronomy Domine ; Lucifer Sam ; Matilda Mother ;
Flaming ; Pow R. Toc H. ; Take Up Thy Stethoscope and
Walk ; Interstellar Overdrive ; The Gnome ; Chapter 24 ;
The Scarecrow ; Bike

A Saucerful of Secrets
Columbia. SCX 6258. July 1968
Let There Be More Light ; Remember A Day ; Set The
Controls for the heart of the Sun ; Corporal Clegg ;
A Sauceful of Secrets ; See-Saw ; Jugband Blues

More. Film Soundtrack
Columbia. SCX 6346. July 1969
Cirrus Minor ; The Nile Song ; Crying Song ; Up the
Khyber ; Green is the Colour ; Cymbaline ; Party Sequence ;
Main Theme ; Ibiza Bar ; More Blues ; Quicksilver ;
A Spanish Piece ; Dramatic Theme

Ummagumma. Double Album
Harvest. SHDW 112. November 1969
Astronomy Domine ; Careful with that axe, Eugene ; Set the
Controls for the Heart of the Sun ; A Saucerful of Secretsl
Sysyphus (Parts 1-4) ; Grantchester Meadows ; Special
Species of Small Furry Animals Gathered Together in a
Cave and Grooving with a Pict ; The Narrow Way (Parts
1-3) ; The Grand Vizier's Garden Party (Part 1 : Entrance ;
Part 2 : Entertainment ; Part 3 ; Exit)

Atom Heart Mother
Harvest. SHVL 781. October 1970
Father's Shout ; Breast Milky ; Mother Fore ; Funky Dung ;
Mind Your Throats Please ; Remergence ; If ; Summer 68 ;
Fat Old Sun ; Alan's Psychedelic Breakfast ; Rise and Shine ;
Sunny Side Up ; Morning Glory

continued

142

Relics
Starline. SRS 5071. May 1971
Arnold Layne ; Interstellar Overdrive ; See Emily Play ;
Remember a Day ; Paintbox ; Julia Dream ; Careful with
that Axe, Eugene ; Cirrus Minor ; The Nile Song ;
Biding My Time ; Bike

Meddle
Harvest. SHVL 795. November 1971
One of These Days ; A Pillow of Winds ; Fearless ;
St. Tropez ; Seamus ; Echoes

Obscured by Clouds. Film Soundtrack
Harvest. SHSP 4020. January 1972
Obscured by Clouds ; When you're in ; Burning Bridges ;
The Gold it's in the . . . ; Wots . . . uh the Deal ; Mudmen ;
Childhood's End ; Free Four ; Stay ; Absolutely Curtains

The Dark Side of the Moon
Harvest. SHVL 804. March 1973
Speak to me ; Breathe ; On the Run ; Time ; The Great Gig
in the Sky ; Money ; Us and Them ; Any Colour You Like ;
Brain Damage ; Eclipse

Hipgnosis

Interview reprinted by courtesy of Performance magazine.
Designed by Hipgnosis and George Hardie N.T.A.

Published by Pink Floyd Music Publishers Ltd.,
27 Noel Street, London W1V 3RD.

Order No. AM76704
US ISBN 978-0-8256-2595-4
UK ISBN 978-0-7119-1987-7

Exclusive Distributors:

Music Sales Corporation
257 Park Avenue South, New York, NY 10010, USA.

Music Sales Limited
Distribution Centre, Newmarket Road, Bury St Edmunds, Suffolk IP33 3YB, UK.

Music Sales Pty Limited
20 Resolution Drive, Caringbah, NSW 2229, Australia.

Printed in the EU.